FAITH AND HOPE

I0626419

Steadfast Anchors In a World of Chaos
31-Daily Meditations

Living Dialog MINISTRIES | Be a new creation

Faith and Hope - Steadfast Anchors In a World of Chaos
31-Daily Meditations

© 2025 Living Dialog Ministries
PO Box 15125
Richmond, VA 23227

Published in the United States of America by
Living Dialog Ministries, a 501(c)(3) tax exempt organization.
www.livingdialog.org

ISBN 979-8-992948-1-5

v. 01
Printed in the United States of America

Text by Jack Dannemiller
Cover and interior design by Brian Regrut

FAITH AND HOPE
Steadfast Anchors in a World of Chaos

31 Daily Meditations

> *"I have told you these things so that in me, you will have peace. In this world, you will have trouble; but take heart, because I have overcome the world."*
> John 16:33

Jesus' words spoken 2000 years ago are just as important for us today. In our chaotic world where there is so much uncertainty about tomorrow, we each need to experience God's peace. So that we are not distracted by the world, it is essential for believers to daily pursue time with God; to be secure in Him and His inspired Word. These 31 Daily Meditations contain readings that are designed to encourage you to remain focused on Jesus Christ and God's promises as we anchor each day in passages from God's Word.

The apostle Paul reminds us that as Christians we are in a spiritual battle with the powers of darkness. As we commit our lives to honor and glorify God, and to build His kingdom the devil and his powers of darkness will come against us. Despite the opposition we are called to fulfill the Great Commission and to become ambassadors for Jesus in all things.

He said to them, "Go into all the world and preach the gospel to all creation. Mark 16:15

Each of you should use whatever gift you have received to serve others, as faithful stewards of God's grace in its various forms.
1 Peter 4:10

Our responsibility is to share the 'good news' that salvation is by God's Grace alone, through Faith alone, in Christ alone. In our daily battles, we must remember that our only defense is the Word of God, the sword of the Spirit. To be equipped each day, we must commit to spending time with the Lord in his Word and being instructed by the Holy Spirit. God can use believers for His purpose when we submit to His will remembering that,

---

*"Greater is He that is in you
than he that is in the world."* 1 John 4:4

We suggest that before you read each day's meditation, take two minutes of silence to prepare your mind and your heart to hear the Lord speak to you. In other words, be like the prophet, Samuel, and say, " Here am I Lord, your servant is listening." After you finish reading the scripture and the meditation, take two more minutes of silence to reflect on what you heard God say. Then make note of it by responding to the questions in the space provided.

Your friends at the Living Dialog ministry thank you for joining us on our journey through God's Word, the Bible. We pray that this collectionof meditations will equip you, strengthen you and bless you each day.

Shalom,
Jack Dannemiller

FAITH

As you enter a time of meditation, reflect on these words:

"Be still, and know that I am God" Psalm 46:10.

Heed this call to inner quiet
and recognition of God's presence and power,
especially in times of chaos or uncertainty.

Allow God's peace to embrace you as you trust in God.
Stop your restless activities and simply be
present, knowing that God is in control.

*For this very reason, make every effort to add
to your faith goodness; and to goodness, knowledge;
and to knowledge, self-control;
and to self-control perseverance;
and to perseverance, godliness; and to godliness,
mutual affection; and to mutual affection, love.*
2 Peter 1:5-7

THE GREATEST OF THESE IS LOVE

For many of us, the first scripture verse we were taught was:

*For God so loved the world that he gave his one and only Son, that
whoever believes in him shall not perish but have eternal life.*

John 3:16

This love is the heart of the gospel. As Christians, we understand that God's love for us was so great that his son, Jesus, was willing to leave the splendor of Heaven to come to a fallen world and die on a Roman cross for our sins. He demonstrated a love that is beyond comprehension. God wants to restore a relationship with men and women that Adam and Eve had broken in the Garden of Eden. God's desire for this restored relationship is so great that he wants us to tell others that the path to restoration is now available to all. He empowers us through the Holy Spirit to share this good news so that others might respond to God's call and be brought into the Kingdom of God.

In today's passage, we observe a profound expression of what God desires for us—to become more like Jesus each day. That process is called sanctification, transforming us from our old self governed by sin to a new creation governed by love. Along this journey, the Holy Spirit teaches us, instructs us, counsels us, gives us wisdom, watches over us, and provides so much more. In response to God's many blessings and promises, we will want to honor Him with our work and our lives, serve him with the gifts and talents He has given us, and enjoy His presence now and forever. We trust that this daily meditation encourages you to trust in God's saving power and His love and that your faith and hope will be strengthened and anchored in the Eternal Rock of your salvation, Jesus Christ.

PRAYER

Gracious Heavenly Father, you will always be my eternal rock and my salvation. May I find comfort and peace today in your Divine Providence and Love that endures forever and never fails. In Jesus' name, Amen!

TODAY'S READING: 2 PETER 1:1-11

What thoughts come to your mind when you meditate on God's great love for you?

How can you become more like Jesus today and every day?

THE ETERNAL ROCK

The scripture for today reminds us that our faith is on a firm foundation. Isaiah declares that the Lord* (YHWH) himself is the Rock. From eternity past until the end of time that Rock will never be shaken. Jesus, God made flesh who lived among us and died to pay the penalty for our sins, is that Rock. Through his death and resurrection we have assurance of eternal life. That assurance is desperately needed in today's troubled times. God's promises are true. He will walk with us even when we face the darkest hours in this life, and one day He will bring us to his heavenly home that we may enjoy life as it was meant to be—free of pain, suffering, guilt, shame and death. God, who has proved to be faithful from creation of the universe, is the one we can trust without any reservation. This solid Rock, on which we as Christ-followers stand, is the basis of our faith. He has overcome the world.

PRAYER

Dear God, my Heavenly Father, I place my trust in you and your word that you are the eternal Rock and the firm foundation of my faith. Help me to trust you with all my heart and soul and mind and to share these words of truth with everyone that you bring into my life journey today.   In Jesus' name, Amen!

*The term Lord in all caps is often used as a substitute for the Hebrew YHWH, which is the sacred four-letter name of God in the Hebrew Bible. The standard "Lord" (sometimes with a lowercase "l") is used to translate the Hebrew word "Adonai," which means "my Lord" and is a common title of respect, or a title used for kings.

When you reflect on Jesus, being the Rock of your faith, how does that bring you peace?

_____

_____

_____

_____

_____

_____

_____

_____

How do the words from Isaiah today strengthen your faith?

_____

_____

_____

_____

_____

_____

_____

_____

What concerns are you facing today that you need to place in the Lord's hands?

_____

_____

_____

_____

_____

And without faith it is impossible to please God, because anyone who comes to him must believe that he exists and that he rewards those who earnestly seek him.
Hebrews 11: 6

FAITH LEADS TO RIGHTEOUSNESS

Today, we started our meditation with selected words from Hebrews 11, what is known as the 'Great Faith' chapter. Here we read about the heroes of the faith, including Abel, Enoch, Noah, Abraham, Isaac, Jacob, Sarah, Joseph and Moses. These people were still living by faith when they died. They did not receive the things promised but they, like us, saw them and welcomed them from a distance. They were longing for a better country—a heavenly one—where there will be no more death or mourning, no more crying or pain for the old order of things will have passed away and God is making all things new (Revelation 21:4). Their faith was counted for them as righteousness before God. Like these heroes, we can look forward with confidence also to our eternal home, a heavenly one, the paradise promised by Jesus. Therefore, if you have placed your trust in Jesus, you can know for sure that your eternal destiny is secure, and that Jesus' righteousness has been applied to you.

PRAYER

Dear Father God, although we cannot see Heaven, we know it is there because you have promised one day to take us with you to your Father's house with many rooms, so that we can also be with you and our loved ones for all eternity. Thank you for that blessed assurance and for your gift of grace that saved us. In Jesus' name, Amen!

How does your faith lead you to righteousness?

_____
_____
_____
_____
_____
_____
_____

When you think of the "heroes of the faith" what is it about their faith that encourages you?

_____
_____
_____
_____
_____
_____

Why can you be confident that your eternal home will be in Heaven?

_____
_____
_____
_____
_____
_____
_____

Now faith is confidence in what we hope for
and assurance about what we do not see.
Hebrews 11:1

LIVE BY FAITH

The word "faith" appears repeatedly in the Scriptures. Jesus said, "If you have faith, you can move mountains" (Matthew 17:20). So, what does the word faith really mean? Webster's dictionary defines faith as "complete trust and confidence in someone or something." Our scripture for today provides one of the biblical definitions of faith. We have confidence in what we hope for because our hope is based on the truth of the Scriptures and in Jesus Christ, who said, "Trust in God; trust also in me" (John 14:1).

We have assurance of Heaven that we don't yet see because Jesus has informed us about it and has given us a sneak preview of it as revealed to the Apostle John and recorded for us in Revelation. Faith can also be defined as the deeply held belief and trust that God will keep His promises. What is unique about our Christian faith, which makes it dependable, is that it is anchored in Jesus Christ and God's Word. So dear friend, live each day with confidence by trusting in Jesus and knowing for certain that your faith is rock solid because Jesus is who He said He is: the Son of God, the Promise Maker, and the Promise Keeper.

PRAYER

Dear Heavenly Father, I thank you for all your promises. Help me to live by faith and have the absolute assurance that you keep all your promises. Thank you that I have the certainty of my eternal destination in Heaven through Jesus Christ my Savior. In Jesus' name, Amen!

Why can you have confidence now in what you hope for?

_____

_____

_____

_____

_____

_____

When have you experienced glimpses of Heaven during your life? How have they impacted your faith?

_____

_____

_____

_____

_____

_____

What about your faith assures you that God will keep his promises?

_____

_____

_____

_____

_____

_____

EVERYONE LIVES BY FAITH

Many people claim they only believe in what they can see or touch. For them, only material reality exists. However, that's not true; everyone lives by faith in something or someone, whether they admit it or not. We all trust planes, or we wouldn't fly. We have faith in elevators, or we wouldn't use them. Therefore, having faith isn't the issue; everyone possesses faith. What makes our Christian faith unique is the person in whom we place our trust: Jesus Christ and God's word.

Why Jesus? Because he is who he claimed to be! He is the Son of God, the Christ and Redeemer, the prophesied Messiah, who forgives sins and offers a way to heaven and eternal life. Jesus promises anyone who trusts in him the assurance of a life-transforming, personal, intimate relationship. Faith in Jesus Christ is the best way to live and the only safe way to die. So today, take time to grow in your relationship with Jesus. You will find peace with God and personal fulfillment in a world and culture filled with chaos and evil. Stay focused on the things above and not on the things below.

PRAYER

Dear Lord, thank you for being the one in whom my faith is anchored. O blessed Jesus, set me securely on your foundation that by your grace I may be found faithful. In Jesus' name, Amen!

What does it mean for you to live by faith?

_____
_____
_____
_____
_____
_____
_____

What or who is the object of your faith? Why?

_____
_____
_____
_____
_____
_____
_____

How does your faith bring your life contentment and fulfillment?

_____
_____
_____
_____
_____
_____

FAITH DAY 6 HOPE

In you, Lord, I have taken refuge... Be my rock of refuge, to which I can always go; give the command to save me, for you are my rock and my fortress.
Psalms 71:1&3

CHRIST THE SOLID ROCK

Faith in Jesus is secure because He is the Solid Rock, the rock of our salvation, our refuge, and the foundation of the Christian faith. As the old gospel hymn says, "all other ground is sinking sand." So, why should we follow Jesus instead of anyone else? Today, we explore some of the reasons why we can place our faith in and trust our lives to the one who is the Solid Rock. Jesus is the only one who can grant you peace with God. In John's gospel, we read the words of Jesus:

"I have told you these things so that in me you will have peace."
John 16:33

Jesus is the only one to forgive sin, as he is the 'Lamb of God' who takes away the sins of the world and all those who trust him by faith (John 1:29). Jesus is the one who gives meaning and purpose to life. He is the only way to heaven and eternal life (John 14:6). Jesus is the light of the world and the source of wisdom, grace and love that endures forever. (John 8:12). Christ is the solid rock. Stand confidently in Him today.

PRAYER

Dear Heavenly Father, I thank you for providing a way to discover the meaning and purpose of my life and the certainty of my eternal destiny through the sacrifice of your Only Begotten Son, the Lamb of God, who takes away the sin of the world and my sin. Use me this day for your purpose and your glory. In Jesus' name, Amen!

What is it about Jesus being the 'Solid Rock' that strengthens your faith?

_____

_____

_____

_____

_____

_____

_____

How does Jesus being the 'Solid Rock' bring peace to your mind and soul?

_____

_____

_____

_____

_____

_____

When have you run to the rock? When your faith was being tested? What was the outcome?

_____

_____

_____

_____

_____

_____

_____

FAITH   DAY 7   HOPE

The Lord lives! Praise be to my Rock!
2 Samuel 22:47 & 50

GOD THE ROCK, MY SAVIOR

None of us have absolute control over our life's destiny, even though we might believe we do. We also lack control over the events happening in the world around us. In fact, we must trust in the Lord and rely on His grace. We need to be in God's Word so that it can be a lamp to our feet and a light to our path.

This day and every day, we need to remember that God is not only the unchanging rock in the midst of a chaotic world, but He invites us to build our lives and love on the unshakable Rock of His character, goodness, and promises. Why? Because God is the Promise Maker, the Promise Keeper, and the Light in this world of darkness. You can be assured that God will keep His promises.

PRAYER

Precious Lord, I thank you for being the Promise Maker and the Promise Keeper. I trust by faith that you will keep your promises. Thank you for being the steady rock in this world of chaos. I take heart in the knowledge that you have overcome the world and that all authority in heaven and on earth has been given to you. Inspire me today with your wisdom and guide my life so that I will be a living testimony to you.
In Jesus' name, Amen!

When you think about God being your Rock, How does that manifest itself in your life?

_____

_____

_____

_____

_____

_____

When you meditate on God being your Savior, what thoughts or images come to mind?

_____

_____

_____

_____

_____

_____

What challenges, hurts or concerns are you dealing with? Write them down, lift them up to the Lord in prayer and come back to this page regularly to be reminded of how God is responding to today's petitions.

_____

_____

_____

_____

_____

_____

The Lord is my rock, my fortress and my deliverer; my God is my rock, in whom I take refuge, my shield and the horn of my salvation, my stronghold.   **Psalms 18:2**

THE LORD IS MY ROCK, MY DELIVERER

Today, we return to the Old Testament to once again hear from King David as the Lord delivered him from the hands of his enemies. Saul was pursuing David, causing him to fear for his life. In his distress, he turned to God and affirmed that the Lord was his deliverer and his rock. By faith, he trusted that the Lord would save him.

We learn from this example that when we feel distressed and troubled by the worries of life—failing health, financial concerns, family relations, emotional stress, and uncertainty about our futures—we can follow David's example and turn to the Lord as our refuge. Jesus reminds us not to worry about tomorrow, for tomorrow will take care of itself; each day has enough trouble of its own (Matthew 6:34). He reiterates this point by saying, "Who of you by worrying can add a single hour to your life?" (Luke 12:25). Therefore, live this day and every day worry-free. Trust in the Lord Jesus, who will deliver you and grant you His peace. He is the Rock of your salvation, the source of your comfort, and your assurance of eternal life.

PRAYER

*Gracious God and Heavenly Father,
I thank you that you are my refuge and my deliverer,
and I can rest assured each day that I have no need to
worry or fret because the Lord Jesus will provide all
the answers for my life's concerns.
In Jesus' name. Amen!*

When has Jesus delivered you from the worries of life? Write them here as a reminder that He is your refuge in times of trouble

_____

_____

_____

_____

_____

_____

What hinders you from seeking Jesus, when life's trials appear. Record them here and give them to him and see how He responds.

_____

_____

_____

_____

_____

What are the reasons you are able to live this day worry free?

_____

_____

_____

_____

_____

_____

"For it is by grace you have been saved, through faith-and this is not from yourselves, it is the gift of God."
Ephesians 2:8

FAITH, A GIFT FROM GOD

In Grace Crowell's book *Meditations*, she describes faith as a power beyond all conception. One that brings the believer's pardon, freedom, oneness with Christ, victory through Christ, and eternal life. She goes on to say that faith enables the believer to be an overcomer.

Through faith, we are accepted, justified, and sanctified by God. We can never fully describe faith, yet it abides in the heart of believers and will guide any Christian safely along the journey of life. Faith in Christ brings the Living Water and with it the power to resist the devil. It is this faith that assures our redemption.

So, how can we use this gift to help others build a rock-solid foundation for Christian living? We must diligently study God's word for wisdom and truth. Then, we will be prepared by the Holy Spirit to share that with others. Great joy will follow when you share the gift of faith so that others embrace it and their faith grows from the 'seeds' we have planted.

PRAYER

Dear Lord, Thank you for the gift of Faith. Kindle this faith into a roaring fire that I may live a life of joy overflowing to everyone I meet so they to will want to know you, the author and finisher of our faith. In Jesus' name, Amen!

What does God's grace look like in your life? How and when have you experienced it?

_____
_____
_____
_____
_____
_____
_____
_____
_____
_____

What does it mean to you personally that you have been justified by faith?

_____
_____
_____
_____
_____
_____

Why is studying God's Word so important in your faith journey?

_____
_____
_____
_____
_____
_____

JESUS, THE OBJECT OF OUR FAITH

The person or object of the Christian faith sets it apart from all other religions. In fact, Christianity is not just a religion; it is a faith centered on a personal relationship with Jesus Christ. Other religions are man-made, whereas Christianity is inspired by God.

Why is this significant? Because the person in whom one places their faith ultimately determines their eternal destiny. We can trust our faith in Jesus because He is a relational God who created us to have a personal relationship with Him. Jesus acts as our intercessor and advocate with God, seated at God's right hand, alive now and forever.

Adam walked with God in the Garden at the very beginning, enjoying a perfect relationship with God and a perfect life. Then he sinned by eating the forbidden fruit from the tree of the knowledge of good and evil. From that time on, humanity has been in rebellion against God. Only the birth, death, and resurrection of Jesus provided a means of reconciliation between humanity and God.

Jesus, the object of our faith, departed from earth and now lives at the right hand of God the Father. But someday He will return and take home with Him all who have placed their faith in Him. In the meantime, we can be assured that Jesus loves us unconditionally, and we should strive to trust and love Him in the same way.

Gracious God, thank you for your promise that you love us unconditionally despite our often failures to honor you with our lives, actions, and words. Today, I put my complete trust in you, with the assurance that you created me to have a personal, intimate relationship with you. In Jesus' name, Amen!

TODAY'S READING: EPHESIANS 3:7-19

How do you know for certain that Christianity is not a religion, but a relationship with Jesus Christ?

What does it mean for you that Jesus is your Advocate and Intercessor with God?

Why can you be confident in Jesus' resurrection? What does it imply for you personally?

FAITH

DAY 11

HOPE

*I know whom I have believed and am convinced that
He is able to guard what I have entrusted to Him.*
2 Timothy 1:12

HAVE FAITH IN GOD

Today's thoughts are drawn from one of the great hymns of the Christian faith, *I Know Whom I Have* Believed. Daniel Whittle created the text of the hymn that has encouraged Christians over the ages in their daily journey of faith. The 2nd and 3rd stanzas of the hymn include the following words:

> *"I know not how this saving faith to me He did impart,
> nor how believing in His word brought peace within my heart.*
>
> *I know not how the spirit moves, convincing men of sin,
> revealing Jesus through the word, and creating faith in Him."*

These verses remind us that although we may never fully understand how God's Spirit moves within us, all we need to do is to trust and put our faith in Jesus. Then we can know with certainty that God, by his mighty power, can transform us into the likeness and characteristics of the Lord Jesus Christ. May these precious words bring peace to your heart and soul each day.

PRAYER

Dear Heavenly Father, thank you for inspiring men and women to create hymns that lift our hearts and souls in worship to you...Words that encourage us in our daily walk ... Words that bring joy and peace and assurance of your love for us. Help me to be more like the Lord Jesus each day and to be faithful and in telling others about Him and your love for each person that I encounter. In Jesus' name, Amen!

How has believing in God's Word brought you peace of mind?

What about the words of this hymn encourages you today?

How has God's power transformed you into the likeness of the Lord Jesus? Which of His attributes do you desire the most?

DAY 12

And he (Christ) died for all, that those who live should no longer live for themselves, but for him who died for them, and was raised again.
2 Corinthians 5:15

LIVING THE CHRISTIAN FAITH

In his letter to the Corinthian church, the Apostle Paul tells us why and how we are to live as Christians. The why is because Christ's love compels us to do so. Paul message was quite clear to all who would listen. He kept it simple so it would be easy to understand. Basically, he preached Christ crucified for our sins and resurrected to demonstrate that in him, one could gain eternal life.

While we cannot all be as accomplished or articulate as Paul, out of love for the Lord Jesus, we are to share the gospel's good news and our personal testimony as living examples of the Christian faith. Are you proud to be a Christian? When God uses you to do great things, you should not be quiet. Proclaiming what God has done in your life is a testimony to the goodness and love of God.

We are inclined to brag about our children or our accomplishments, but God wants us to tell others about him and his great love for his children and for the lost. Living the Christian faith can sometimes be a daunting task, and we may even experience persecution for standing firm for Jesus. The good news is that, in all circumstances, God promises never to leave us or forsake us and that he will give us the strength and wisdom for the good works he planned for each of us before the foundation of the world.

All we need to do each day is to ask and rest assured that God is always faithful and answers our prayers according to his perfect will.

Dear Heavenly Father: Thank you for hearing and answering my prayers. Please give me strength for each day and uphold me with your righteous right hand so that I may be about doing the good works you have planned for me so that you receive the praise and the honor and the glory. Help me to live out my Christian faith so that others will see Jesus in me and want to come to know him. In Jesus' name, Amen!

TODAY'S READING: 2 CORINTHIANS 5:1-15

When recently, have you shared the gospel's Good news with a friend? How was it received?

_____

_____

_____

_____

What aspects of your Christian testimony do you consider the most important to share?

_____

_____

_____

What wisdom do you need from God today to carry out his plan for you?

_____

_____

_____

_____

Jesus said, "Let the little children come to me, and do not hinder them, for the Kingdom of God belongs to such as these."   **Matthew 19:14**

FAITH AS A LITTLE CHILD

These precious words of Jesus echo through the corridors of time to us today. In Jesus' time, little children were not given much attention. Did you notice that in responding to the disciples' suggestion that the children be ignored, Jesus added the word "little" to describe the children who came to him? The teaching for us is that little children are completely dependent on their parents. They also have absolute trust in both their father and mother. In other words, to have faith like a little child means that we are to be wholly dependent on our Heavenly Father for every need in our lives and to trust him in every circumstance. When you accept Jesus as your Lord and Savior, you become a child of God, adopted into His family. You have the awesome privilege of approaching God as ABBA Father, Daddy. In this special relationship, He will supply our every need and He will never leave us or forsake us. So, where in your life do you need to trust God more to enjoy an intimate relationship with Him as your Heavenly Father? He's already holding you in His everlasting arms, lean into His embrace so that you can enjoy His presence now and forever.

PRAYER

Loving Heavenly Father: Thank you for your continual embrace, welcoming me into your presence daily. I am blessed with the privilege of calling you ABBA, Father, and Daddy. Thank you for your assurance that you will meet all my needs according to the glorious riches in Christ Jesus. Help me to trust you more and share your love with everyone.
In Jesus' name, Amen!

What can you do to depend more on God and trust Him more completely?

_____

_____

_____

_____

_____

_____

What is it you need to ask of your Heavenly Father today? Write it here and watch for His answer as you bring it to him in prayer?

_____

_____

_____

_____

_____

When do you enjoy most being in God's presence? Is He your first thought every morning?

_____

_____

_____

_____

_____

_____

_____

Jesus said, "Do not worry about tomorrow, for tomorrow, will worry about itself. Each day has enough trouble of its own."   Matthew 6:34

FAITH, A DAY AT A TIME

Scripture reminds us repeatedly to have faith in God and not to be afraid or discouraged. Jesus teaches us that faith is the absolute certainty that God will keep His promises. We are also reminded by Jesus to take heart because He has overcome the world. This confidence enables us not to worry or feel anxious about what lies ahead. God is sovereign in all things, including our plans and activities. "One Day at a Time" is a well-known Christian song whose lyrics echo the theme of today's meditation:

One day at a time, sweet Jesus, that's all I'm asking from You."
   Lord, give me the strength to do every day for what I have to do
Yesterday's gone, sweet Jesus, and tomorrow may never be mine.
   Lord help me today, show me the way, one day at a time.

We encourage you to find this song online and listen to it. The music and message will uplift you and help you live without worry, One Day at a Time.

PRAYER

Dear Jesus: It is with a grateful heart that I come into your presence today to thank you for all of your words of encouragement so that I can live worry-free each day because you have overcome the world. Strengthen my faith so that I can live according to your perfect will, one day at a time. In your name, I pray. Amen!

What concern or worry do you need to give to Lord today?

_____

_____

_____

_____

_____

_____

What promises of God's are you absolutely certain he will keep? What are most precious for you?

_____

_____

_____

_____

_____

How do the lyrics of the song, "One day at a time sweet Jesus" encourage you today?

_____

_____

_____

_____

_____

Jesus said to his disciples," For whoever wants to save their life, will lose it, but whoever loses their life for me, and for the gospel will save it. What good is it for someone to gain the whole world and forfeit their soul."
Mark 8:35-36

SOUL SAVING FAITH

When a crowd had gathered around Jesus and his disciples, Jesus seized the opportunity to teach them an important lesson. That same truth speaks to us today, reminding us that it is through faith in Jesus that our souls are saved. He went on to teach them that if anyone is ashamed of him and his words, the Son of Man, Jesus, will be ashamed of them when he comes into his Father's glory with the holy angels.

Our soul-saving faith is assured when we place it in Jesus, the unshakable, eternal rock. The cross was the price Jesus paid for our salvation. When he declared, "It is finished" (John 19:30), it meant that the debt had been paid for the sins of all those who, by faith, trusted in him. So, live this day filled with joy and the assurance of heaven and eternal life you have because of your faith in his sacrifice for you.

PRAYER

Loving Jesus: Thank you for paying the debt from my sins, so that I can live my life, trusting in you, with the absolute assurance that I am saved. Thank you for showing me that I will spend eternity in your presence with my loved ones, and the saints of the ages.
In your precious name I pray. Amen!

What does it mean to you that in Jesus, your eternal soul is saved?

_____
_____
_____
_____
_____
_____
_____

When you meditate on Jesus, being the unshakable, eternal rock, what images come to mind?

_____
_____
_____
_____
_____

What thoughts do you have when you realize that Jesus paid for your sin in full at the cross?

_____
_____
_____
_____
_____
_____

FAITH **DAY 16** HOPE

*"Therefore, do not worry about tomorrow,
for tomorrow will worry about itself.
Each day has enough trouble of its own."*
Matthew 6:34

FAITH IN JESUS DEFEATS WORRY

For many, anxiety is a constant companion. What do you worry about? Relationships? A job? Finances? The state of our culture? God knows and understands your concerns. That's why He wants you to cast your cares on Him. (1 Peter 5:7) How do you do that? A hymn written more than 100 years ago answers this question:

O soul, are you weary and troubled? No light in the darkness you see?
There's light for a look at the Savior, and life more abundant and free!
Turn your eyes upon Jesus, Look full in His wonderful face,
And the things of earth will grow strangely dim,
In the light of His glory and grace.

As today's scripture tells us, we are not to fret about the future because it is in God's hands, not ours. When you fully trust Jesus each day, you'll find that your worries will be lifted and your anxiety lessened because Jesus has reassured us that He is in control. Remember, Jesus said, "Take heart; I have overcome the world" (John 16:33).

PRAYER

Lord Jesus: Thank you for your words of assurance that you are in control and I do not need to worry about tomorrow. Take away the anxiety that prevents me from living my life for you. Help me trust in you each day to provide the strength for every task and wisdom for each decision I make. May all that I do and say glorify and honor you. I ask this in your name, Amen!

What are you worrying about today? Write it down in the space provided and give it to Jesus. He is willing to bear your griefs and sins.

Have you asked Jesus for strength today? What task do you need his help to accomplish? Write your request here and offer it to him in prayer.

How did the lyrics of the hymn resonate with you?

HOPE

JESUS IS OUR STEADFAST HOPE

Today, we will shift our focus and thoughts to the word "hope." It serves as the second anchor in our absolute trust in Jesus Christ, the eternal rock of our salvation. First, we must recognize that biblical hope describes something different from the type of hope we discuss in everyday language. It is not the "hope" of winning the lottery or expecting to wake up in the morning and no longer need glasses to read. Biblical hope is a desire of the heart and a conviction of faith—knowing with certainty that what is desired is attainable. Real hope, steadfast hope, must, therefore, be based on something that has proven over time to be real and trustworthy. God's Word, the Bible, tells us that this hope is found in Jesus Christ and in the promises of God.

We will explore this truth in more depth in the days ahead. God has given us His promises to encourage our hearts, and nothing will lift your weary soul or give you more hope than the promises of God. So, stand firm on His promises and live this day with the absolute assurance that God will keep His promises. Remember, the Lord Himself goes before you and will be with you; He will never leave you nor forsake you. (Deuteronomy 31:8)

PRAYER

Dear Heavenly Father: Thank you that we can stand firm and have confident hope in your promises. You are the Promise Maker and the Promise Keeper. You have promised never to leave me or forsake me. Please give me the confidence to trust in this promise and live faithfully and boldly for you each day. In Jesus' name, Amen!

When you reflect on today's scripture, what does it mean for you to put your hope in Jesus?

_____

_____

_____

_____

_____

_____

How has God's Word spoken to your heart and given you hope in times of trial?

_____

_____

_____

_____

_____

_____

What gives you confidence that the Lord himself goes before you and will be with you, and will never leave you or for you?

_____

_____

_____

_____

_____

_____

DAY 18

Israel, put your Hope in the Lord, for with the Lord is unfailing love and with him is full redemption.
Psalm 130:7

PUT YOUR HOPE IN THE LORD

Today's Scripture is not only for the nation of Israel but also for all those who call upon the name of the Lord and have been adopted into God's family. It is for those of us who have become children of God through our faith in Jesus Christ as Lord and Savior. The Bible tells us that God is love and that His love endures forever and never fails. That love of God is reflected in the gift of Jesus, His only begotten Son, through whom alone we can receive redemption from sin and have the assurance of eternal life and the ultimate destiny of the paradise of Heaven. As we trust in God's love and goodness, He assures us of both our redemption and full restoration. The Holy Spirit will reveal a future where hope is possible.

So, trust in the Lord with all your heart and lean not on your own understanding; in all your ways acknowledge Him, and He will make your path straight and your future secure. Proverbs 3:5-6

PRAYER

Lord Jesus: Help me to completely trust in you and not in my knowledge but in your wisdom. Holy Spirit teach me and instruct me in God's ways so that I always walk in the path of righteousness and in His will. In your name I pray. Amen!

When you meditate on this scripture from the Psalms, in what ways does it assure you that You have been redeemed?

_____
_____
_____
_____
_____
_____

Where have you experienced God's grace and love recently? How has that impacted your trust and hope in God?

_____
_____
_____
_____
_____
_____

How can you trust more in the Lord today and not depend on your own understanding?

_____
_____
_____
_____
_____

*Those who Hope in the L*ord *will renew their strength.*
They will soar on wings like eagles, they will run and
not be weary, they will walk and not be faint.
Isaiah 40:31

HOPE IN THE PROMISES OF GOD

The Bible contains over 7,000 promises that God makes for His children. Some of the promises are specific to the nation of Israel, but most are for those who have placed their trust in Jesus as their Savior. Today's scripture is one that should bring you joy and excitement as you contemplate soaring on wings like eagles, running without becoming weary, and walking while never feeling tired.

Have you ever observed a pair of eagles soaring on thermals? They don't seem to have a care in the world. Their Creator has given them this wonderful ability to fly. This is what God, your Heavenly Father, desires for each of His children. He wants us to soar in the hope and joy that we have in Jesus. Why? Because He is a loving, gracious God who delights in giving extraordinary gifts to His children. You can experience this same joy every day when you hope in and trust the promises of God.

PRAYER

Dear Heavenly Father: Thank you for your many promises. Please remind me each day to trust in you and your promises so that I can have the joy of soaring on wings like eagles and running the race of life in the strength and hope that you alone provide.
In Jesus' name, Amen!

How will today's scripture help you soar like Eagles and bring joy to your life?

_____
_____
_____
_____
_____
_____
_____

What circumstances have disappointed you recently? How will meditating on Isaiah 40:31 enable you to find hope to overcome these disappointments?

_____
_____
_____
_____
_____
_____
_____

How do the promises of God give you hope and keep you from becoming weary?

_____
_____
_____
_____
_____
_____

PLACE YOUR HOPE IN GOD ALONE

We all have days when things don't go as planned. When plans go awry, it's easy to feel discouraged and downcast. There are days when life's challenges and the chaos of the world can disturb our souls. So, what can we do to overcome our frustration and discouragement?

The Psalmist encourages us to put our hope in God, and He will lift our spirits when we praise Him. We can praise Him with our words and by lifting our voices and hearts in song. The worship song, Because He Lives, includes lyrics that inspire joyful praise. Hear these words of hope in the song's chorus:

> *Because He lives, I can face tomorrow.*
> *Because he lives, all fear is gone.*
> *Because I know He holds the future,*
> *Life is worth the living just because He lives.*

May these words of praise be yours today.

PRAYER

Heavenly Father: My hope is in you and your precious promises. In you alone I trust to help me keep from being discouraged and downcast.
Because you live I can face tomorrow knowing that you have overcome the world and are in control.
In Jesus name, Amen!

What is causing discontent in your life? What are some practical
steps you can take to become content and not be discouraged?

_____

_____

_____

_____

_____

_____

_____

When did you last praise God for his many blessings? Why not
memorize this song's words and offer them daily to the Lord?

_____

_____

_____

_____

_____

_____

How does the fact that Jesus lives inspire you today?

_____

_____

_____

_____

_____

_____

May the God of Hope fill you with all joy and peace as you trust in him, so that you may overflow with hope by the power of the Holy Spirit.
Romans 15:13

ABUNDANT HOPE

The letter of the Apostle Paul to the believers in Rome, both Jews and Gentiles, is as relevant today as it was 2,000 years ago. His message for them and for us was revolutionary. God chose to create a new worldwide family through faith in Jesus. That family is the Church, the body of Christ, comprised of believers in Jesus as Savior.

Through the power of the Holy Spirit, lives are transformed, and one becomes a new creation. This new life as a believer breaks the stronghold of sin and evil. It assures you of abundant and overflowing hope for joy and peace in this life, along with the absolute certainty of eternal life. So, place your hope today in the One whose kingdom is eternal. He will never disappoint you. His love endures forever.

PRAYER

Loving Heavenly Father: Please fill me with joy and peace by the power of the Holy Spirit. Thank you for adopting me into your family. May all that I do honor you so that I can enjoy your presence now and forever. In Jesus' name, Amen!

What does it mean to you that in Jesus, your eternal soul is saved?

_____

_____

_____

_____

_____

_____

_____

When you meditate on Jesus, being the unshakable, eternal rock, what images come to mind?

_____

_____

_____

_____

_____

_____

What thoughts do you have when you realize that Jesus paid your sin that in full at the cross?

_____

_____

_____

_____

_____

_____

The Lᴀᴀᴀ is good to those who Hope in Him.
Lamentations 3:25

HOPE IN THE GOODNESS OF GOD

The Book of Lamentations is attributed to the prophet Jeremiah. It was written to those left behind in Jerusalem after the Babylonian conquest in 586 BC. They were in great despair, having suffered catastrophic losses and enduring deep grief and immense suffering. This collection of laments reminds us that experiencing anguish over life's sorrows and disappointments is to be expected in a fallen world affected by sin.

The good news for us today is that Jesus has overcome the world (John 16:33), and we can experience the Lord's goodness and peace when we hope in Him. So today, place your hope in the Lord with the certainty that He is good—all the time. Even in the midst of our difficulties and disappointments, we are assured that the Lord remains good.

PRAYER

Dear Heavenly Father: Help me this day to experience anew your goodness as I Hope in you, trust in your word and in your unfailing love that endures forever. Thank you, Lord Jesus, for reminding me that you have overcome the world and in you I will have peace.
In your name, Amen!

How have you experienced God's goodness this past week?

_____

_____

_____

_____

_____

What causes disappointments and discontent in your life?
What are some steps you can take to become more content?

_____

_____

_____

_____

_____

_____

What are you doing to strengthen your hope and your soul today?

_____

_____

_____

_____

_____

*May your unfailing love be with us LORD,
even as we put our hope in you.*
Psalm 33:22

HOPE IN GOD'S UNFAILING LOVE

Psalm 33 is a prayer that petitions God to bless us with His unfailing love. The Scriptures remind us not to love the world, as its desires and attractions will fade away; however, those who love the Lord will experience His love and live forever. The Psalms were used in worship, expressing praise and exaltation of a God of hope. Though written over 2,500 years ago, these psalms continue to inspire songwriters. Many contemporary Christian praise songs incorporate the words and sentiments expressed in the Psalms. These verses have provided comfort, inspiration, and hope to God's people in every era and on every continent. Millions have memorized these psalms, particularly those written by King David. His 23rd psalm, "The Lord is my Shepherd," is among the most beloved of all scriptures. In total, the collection of 150 Psalms documents and celebrates God's plan throughout history to save His people and all those today who place their hope and trust in Jesus as Savior. You can be assured that when you hope in the Lord, He will renew your strength. You will receive His guidance and enjoy His presence now and forever. You can have confident hope for your future because of God's unconditional love.

Prayer

*Merciful Heavenly Father: Thank you for your
unconditional love that never fails and lasts forever.
I will trust in you to provide my strength for each day
so that your will be done in my life and that you will
receive the honor and the glory. In Jesus' name, Amen!*

How can you express your love for the Lord in new ways this week? With whom do you need to share God's love?

_____

_____

_____

_____

_____

_____

_____

How does this Psalm provide you with hope for every circumstance in life?

_____

_____

_____

_____

_____

_____

When have you experienced God's unfailing love? How did He give you strength and hope for your future?

_____

_____

_____

_____

_____

_____

REST IN GOD MY ROCK

Psalm 65 is another song written by King David. It was offered to the director of music to be sung in worship of God. In it, David expresses his confidence in God alone for his salvation and peace of soul. He also implores the Israelites to trust in God at all times—during both good and bad moments and in every circumstance. David's message resonates with us today. It reminds us not to place our hope in worldly riches or to set our hearts on the enticing promises of our culture. The things of this world will ultimately disappoint us and fade away, but those who trust in the Lord will live forever. Jesus affirmed this truth:

"No one can serve two masters. Either you will hate one and love the other, or you will be devoted to one and despise the other. You can not serve both God and money." Luke 16:13

So, in your life journey, keep your eyes on Jesus, the author and perfecter of your faith, and put your faith and trust in God, not in the things of the world. God will never disappoint you.

PRAYER

Dear Jesus: Help me keep my eyes on you and inspire me to be about the 'good works' planned for me before the foundation of the world. Amen!

Are you following the world and its culture instead of the Word of God? If you ask Him today to help you live according to the Spirit, how will your life be transformed?

_____

_____

_____

_____

_____

_____

How can you become a more faithful steward of the time, talents and treasures God has entrusted to you?

_____

_____

_____

_____

_____

What do you need to do to keep your eyes focused more on Jesus?

_____

_____

_____

_____

_____

_____

LOOKING TO OUR HOPE IN CHRIST

These words from the Apostle Paul to the church in Ephesus speak to the church today and to every believer in Jesus, encouraging us to keep our hearts focused and our eyes open so that we can be assured of our eternal hope in Christ. Paul reminds believers in Rome:

> *And we know that in all things God works for the good of those who love him, who have been called according to his purpose.*
> Romans 8:28

As a Christian, you can be assured that God called you to an eternal Hope, which is your "guarantee" of a life with meaning and purpose and the certainty of your eternal destiny in Heaven. Remember, God will keep his word to those he calls his children. May your faith be anchored in the Hope that God alone provides.

PRAYER

Dear Heavenly Father: Thank you for calling us to be your children and for your Amazing Grace, which enlightens our hearts so that we can be confident that our Hope is secure in Jesus. In His name, Amen!

What purpose do you believe God has planned for you? How have you experienced the 'Good' in your life?

_____

_____

_____

_____

_____

_____

_____

Are you certain that you have eternal life? Have you trusted in Jesus as your Savior? Write down the date that you first believed, and received assurance of of your salvation.

_____

_____

_____

_____

What does it mean for you to be a child of God?

_____

_____

_____

_____

_____

"May the God of Hope fill you with all joy and peace as you trust in him, so that you may overflow with Hope by the power of the Holy Spirit"
Romans 15:13

HOPE IN THE HOLY SPIRIT'S POWER

Hope is defined as a feeling of expectation and the desire for something to happen, grounds for believing something good will occur. The Bible assures followers of Jesus that they should expect good life experiences as they trust in the God of hope in the power of the Holy Spirit to provide blessings that overflow. That does not necessarily mean that life will be trouble-free. Christians can expect life to have its trials, temptations, and disappointments. In the Gospel of John 16:33, Jesus reminds us that we will have trouble in this world, but he encourages us to take heart because He has overcome the world.

This promise gives us Hope to live a life worthy of our calling as a child of God and an ambassador for Christ. Whatever trials you are experiencing, when your Hope is in Jesus, God will always be there and love you forever.

PRAYER

Holy Spirit: I thank you that you are my intercessor and that as a child of God, you live within me, and by your power, I will be able to overcome the temptations of life and endure the trials that may come my way. Please enable me always to be a faithful ambassador of the gospel of the Lord Jesus Christ.
In Jesus' name, Amen!

How have you seen the Holy Spirit's power at work in your life?

_____

_____

_____

_____

_____

_____

_____

_____

_____

What does it mean for you that Jesus has overcome the world?

_____

_____

_____

_____

_____

_____

_____

How has the Holy Spirit helped you overcome temptation?

_____

_____

_____

_____

_____

_____

"I know the plans I have for you," declares the LORD,
*"plans to prosper you and not to harm you, plans to
give you Hope and a future.*
Jeremiah 29:11

HOPE IN THE LORD'S PLANS

Scripture teaches us that God has prepared a plan of 'good works' for us to accomplish during our lives. This plan was established even before we were born. Because our Heavenly Father is a relational God, He desires for our lives to have meaning and purpose and for us to partner with Him. We can achieve this only by discovering His will through prayer and the study of the Bible.

Those plans become a reality when we engage in a personal, life-transforming relationship with the Lord Jesus Christ. God has given us the Holy Spirit to guide and counsel us as we pursue fulfilling His plan for our lives. Therefore, as we navigate life according to God's will, His plan offers us hope for each day and the assurance of a fulfilling future. So, embrace this day and every day by trusting God for His guidance and wisdom. Utilize the talents He has given you to accomplish the 'good works' that build God's kingdom.

PRAYER

*Gracious God: Thank you for preparing a plan for my life even before the foundations of the world were put into place. As I search your Word, please reveal your good, pleasing, and pleasant will for me. I look forward to each day being about accomplishing the exciting plan you have for my life.
In Jesus' name, Amen!*

When you think about the 'good works', God has planned for you, what have you experienced?

_____

_____

_____

_____

_____

_____

_____

What 'good work' has excited you the most? Being a loving spouse? Raising a family? Teaching a Bible class for children, youth or adults? Excelling in a profession? A passion for reaching the lost?

_____

_____

_____

_____

_____

_____

How are you finding Hope in the Lord's plans for you this day? ?

_____

_____

_____

_____

_____

*Brothers and sisters, we do not want you
to be uninformed about those who sleep in death
so that you do not grieve like the rest of mankind,
who have no Hope.*
1 Thessalonians 4:13

HOPE GREATER THAN OUR GRIEF

Ever since men and women understood the concept of death, they have asked the question: What happens when I die? Only God offers the true answer to the question. God created mankind in His image because, like all good fathers, he desires a personal relationship with his sons and daughters.

This relationship became strained and broken when individuals decided that they knew better than God, their Heavenly Father, and separated themselves from the only person who ever loved them unconditionally. Their original sin, breaking God's command, brought death to the human race. The good news is that God has offered a redemption plan for all who trust in the Lord Jesus Christ as their Savior. So now, all those who follow Christ have the certainty of eternal life and the destination of heaven when they die. That is the reason that Christians do not grieve in hopelessness at death like the rest of mankind.

Believers in Jesus know that the best is yet to come when this physical life ends. Today, you can have the certainty and blessed assurance of being in God's presence and being reunited with your loved ones for all eternity. And you can be assured that God's grace is always greater than any grief you may experience.

PRAYER

Dear Lord, Thank you for your Amazing Grace, which is greater than my grief. Thank you for loving me unconditionally and providing for my redemption and salvation in your Son, the Lord Jesus Christ. When I experience trouble and sorrow, even death, I will trust in you because I know that you love me and want me to enjoy your presence now and forever. In Jesus' name, Amen!

TODAY'S READING: 1 THESSALONIANS 4:1318

What grief or concern are you wrestling with today that you need to give to the Lord, so that He can bring healing and restore your hope?

_____

_____

_____

_____

_____

_____

How have you experienced God's grace in times of sadness, or in the death of a loved one?

_____

_____

_____

_____

_____

_____

_____

If God is for us, who can be against us?
He who did not spare his own son but gave him up for
us all—how will he not also, along with Him,
graciously give us all things.
Romans 8:31-32

HOPE IN GOD WHO IS FOR US

We have a wonderful message of hope in this scripture from Paul in Romans. First, he reminds us that nothing in this life will ever separate us from the love of God that is in Christ Jesus our Lord. We all face trials and challenges on this journey, but God has promised that He is faithful in all circumstances. When our hope is in the Lord, He will provide the wisdom and strength for our daily needs.

Further along in the passage, Paul lists challenges that could beset us including famine, hardship, persecution, demons, other powers, death, or anything else in all creation. Paul concludes that despite these challenges, when God is for us, we will be overcomers. So, walk confidently each day in the light of God's Word.

You can be assured that He will graciously give you everything you need according to His perfect will. Like a good earthly father, our Heavenly Father loves to provide for His children—those who have trusted in the Lord Jesus as their Savior. Rest assured, God will give strength for today and hope for tomorrow.

PRAYER

Gracious God: Thank you for the promise that
nothing can separate me from your love. Please give
me strength each day so I can conquer the things that
might try to keep me from my confident Hope in you.
In Jesus name, Amen!

What difference does it make in your life that nothing can ever separate you from God's love?

When you face trials and challenges, how does your hope in God give you strength to be an Overcomer?

Where is your Hope found, in God's promises or in the things of the world? If hope is not found in God's promises, what changes do you need to make in your life?

We have this Hope as an anchor for the soul,
firm and secure.   **Hebrews 6:19**

HOPE IN OUR ANCHOR, JESUS OUR HIGH PRIEST

Hebrews was written for the 1st-century Jewish community who believed in Jesus and were at risk of losing their faith in Him. This book resonates with us today just as it did 2,000 years ago. As followers of Jesus, we, too, possess this Hope as an anchor for our souls. It is this hope that strengthens us in our daily walk with the Lord, helping us to avoid distractions from worldly desires and remain steadfast in our faith. It was true then and remains true now that we can have unwavering faith because Jesus is our high priest and intercessor for our prayers and petitions to God, our Heavenly Father.

Therefore, as God's faithful people today, we must continue to live in the light of God's unseen heavenly truths and step out as Christ's ambassadors in faith. In Jesus, you have an anchor for your Hope grounded in His righteousness, and you are receiving a kingdom that cannot be shaken. Remember to thank God each day for His amazing grace and for your adoption into His kingdom as one of His children and a co-heir with Jesus.

PRAYER

Loving Father: Thank you for assuring my eternal destiny in your heavenly Kingdom. Please help me to be a faithful ambassador of the Gospel. Thank you for the certainty that my faith is rock solid and enables me to live daily as Jesus' faithful follower. In Jesus name, Amen!

What does it mean to you that with faith in Jesus, you have an anchor for your eternal soul?

_____

_____

_____

_____

_____

_____

_____

When you meditate on Jesus, being the unshakable, eternal rock, what thoughts come to mind about His being your "High Priest" and intercessor?

_____

_____

_____

_____

_____

_____

_____

What thoughts do you have when you realize that Jesus paid your sin that in full at the cross? What does it mean for you that in Jesus you have an anchor for your Hope?

_____

_____

_____

_____

_____

> *"Therefore, everyone who hears these words of mine and puts them into practice is like a wise man who built his house on the rock. The rain came down, the streams rose, and the winds blew and beat against that house, yet it did not fall because it had its foundations on the rock."*   **Matthew 7:24**

STAND ON CHRIST THE SOLID ROCK

This message from Jesus in Matthew is meant for wise Kingdom builders. These words encourage us to base our lives on Him, the Solid Rock, the foundation of our faith, and the source of our hope, as Jesus is the joy of our salvation. It is entirely fitting that we lift our voices and hearts to Him in song on this 31st day of meditations. There is no more appropriate Christian song to express our worship than "On Christ the Solid Rock I Stand," written in 1834 by Edward Mote. Take a moment to read these timeless words:

> *My hope is built on nothing less than Jesus' blood and righteousness.*
> *I dare not trust the sweetest frame, but holy trust in Jesus' name.*
> *In every rough and stormy gale my anchor holds within the veil.*
> *When all around my soul gives way, he then is still my hope and stay."*
>
> *Refrain: On Christ the solid Rock I stand*
> *All other ground is sinking sand…all other ground is sinking sand.*

This hymn continues to remind us that our faith and hope are in Christ, the Solid Rock. When the storms of life arise, you have an anchor that will hold firm. Debbie McDaniel, a writer whose mission is to encourage others and share hope from God's Word in the daily grind of life, reminds us: "There are many opinions, beliefs, and voices calling to us from the secular culture. We simply need to turn it all off and listen to the One voice—Jesus—who matters most and in whom we place our hope and faith."

*Our Heavenly Father: May your words indeed be a
lamp unto our feet and a light unto our path, guiding
me on my life's journey. I place my Faith and Hope in
the Lord Jesus, the Solid Rock. Please help me to trust
totally in You and be patient while waiting out the
storms of life, knowing that my faith is secure in Jesus,
my Rock. In His name, Amen!*

TODAY'S READING: MATTHEW 7:13-29

Take a close look at today's scripture. Let it really sink in. Now ask
yourself, is my faith truly and confidently based on Christ the
Solid Rock? If not, what should you do to gain that assurance?

Are you trusting in Jesus alone for your salvation? Have you sought
him as your Lord and savior?

MAY THE GOD OF HOPE FILL YOU WITH JOY AND PEACE
NOW AND ALWAYS.

FAITH   AFTERWORDS   HOPE

*Jesus said, "Now this is eternal life; that they may
know you, the only true God and Jesus Christ whom
you have sent."*
John 17:3

Much like the Book of Proverbs, this collection of meditations has been created for repeated use. It is numbered and not dated for a specific month like many other devotional booklets. Our objective was and is to create a booklet that can be reviewed, treasured, and even memorized along your life journey. We at Living Dialog Ministries hope that it will be a publication that will inspire and encourage you for years to come.

Perhaps you received it from a friend or a pastor to point you to a life-transforming, intimate personal relationship with Jesus. The scriptures in this booklet have been chosen for that purpose. They are a reminder of the most incredible love story ever written about the most extraordinary life ever lived, Jesus Christ. The creator God loved this masterpiece of his creation, mankind, so much that he set a plan in motion to provide a way for human beings who turned their back on Him in the garden of Eden to be restored and into fellowship —a fellowship that will last throughout all eternity.

This simply means that when you have an intimate, personal relationship with Jesus as your Lord and Savior, you have a new life now and a promise of a better one forever. Then, you will experience an abundant and exciting adventure with the one through whom God created the universe. If you don't already know for certain that your eternal life is secure in Christ Jesus, and you want to experience this abundant life you have been reading about, take a few minutes to ask God to forgive your sins.

Accept his pardon and understand that Jesus died in your place. You can do this by praying a simple prayer in your own words like this:

Lord Jesus: I confess I am a sinner and need you as My Savior. I repent of my sins and invite you into my heart to be Lord of my life. I believe that God raised You from the dead and that You are alive forevermore and seated at God's right hand. Thank you for saving me. With your guidance, I will faithfully follow you all the days of my life. Amen.

You may not necessarily feel any different at the moment, but you can be assured that you have eternal life and one day, you will meet Jesus face to face in heaven. You have become a born-again child of God, this maker of heaven and earth that we proclaim in the Apostles' Creed. Now, begin to experience His peace, love, and amazing grace this and every day. So what is next?

1. To start, we recommend that you acquire a good study Bible, such as the *Life Application Bible, New International Version* (NIV). Then, begin by reading the Gospel of John.

2. When you finish investigating the message in the Gospel of John, go back and read the other accounts of Jesus' life in Matthew, Mark, and Luke, as well as the Acts of the Apostles.

3. When you have read about the lives of the Disciples of Jesus after his death, resurrection, and ascension into Heaven, you'll want to read the letters of Paul and the other Apostles.

4. Then, we recommend you return to the beginning, the book of Genesis, and begin your adventure through the entire Bible.

5. You can also visit our website, LivingDialog.org, to find Study guides, books, and booklets that will encourage you in your faith journey.

6. We also encourage you to find a Christ-centered, Bible-teaching church and attend regularly. You should find an opportunity to participate in Bible studies that will encourage you in your walk with Jesus.

You have embarked upon the most incredible adventure you will ever know. May God bless your reading and understanding of these reflections on being a Christian—to believe in Jesus Christ as your Savior, the Hope for your Faith, and the Rock of your salvation. Amen!